Prasenjit Jana

TIME AND WE

Prasenjit Jana

TIME AND WE

Physical time and thinking time

JustFiction Edition

Imprint
Any brand names and product names mentioned in this book are subject to trademark, brand or patent protection and are trademarks or registered trademarks of their respective holders. The use of brand names, product names, common names, trade names, product descriptions etc. even without a particular marking in this work is in no way to be construed to mean that such names may be regarded as unrestricted in respect of trademark and brand protection legislation and could thus be used by anyone.

Cover image: www.ingimage.com

Publisher:
JustFiction! Edition
is a trademark of
Dodo Books Indian Ocean Ltd. and OmniScriptum S.R.L publishing group

120 High Road, East Finchley, London, N2 9ED, United Kingdom
Str. Armeneasca 28/1, office 1, Chisinau MD-2012, Republic of Moldova, Europe
Printed at: see last page
ISBN: 978-620-0-10441-0

Contents

Preface

This book is for our own time. The book is about the time which we feel. After reading the book no one will waste time. Time is made up by thinking and that helps us. The reader must read the book carefully to find the difference between the physical time and thinking time. I have read books on real time and I mention it as physical time, but the actual time is that which we think about. I am thankful to the publisher who published my paper on time and we. Now I decide to publish a book on it because the actual time is not that which we see. The time is essential for artificial intelligence because the person or the machine which can think faster than the given time is more intelligent than other. So this book is helpful for AI also. I am thankful to my father Sri Basudeb Jana and mother Late Mira Jana for their support and effort for coming out from my bad days. I am proud of my father, mother and brother.

<u>**Time and we**</u>

Time is nothing but the realisation of change of one thing with other. The time is a feeling of change. Those who feel the change very fast can realise the thinking of time and can feel the time very sharp than other. In every position of earth the time is different and for every person the time is different. As the person differs the thinking of change differs and time differs. If the time is same then thinking of different person is same. I am not saying about the time what the earth follows but I am saying that time what we follow. Actually the earth moves around the Sun in 365 days and some hours (approximately) but only someone can use this time as a year. I want to say that for someone it is a year and for someone it is a day may be. I want to say like to an elephant it may be like two years or who feels the time slow can think that it is equal to two years. So different people think the time differently and for that time is different for everyone. If we say that what is then time? The time is the rate of change of a thing with respect to thinking. That is if a clock shows the change (the physical change) of an hour hand then (dt/dT) is the time and also reversely (dT/dt) is the time, where t= time T= thinking.

To understand it better we have to understand two things.

1) Normal time or physical time
2) Absolute time or realising time
1) Normal time or physical time

If we see the clock then we can understand that the clock shows a movement and we find that it is a time.

2) Absolute time or realising time

If we feel that the clock is moving slow or fast as per our work, I want to mean the clock moves but my thinking goes fast and I do the job before the clock moves and I feel that time which is absolute time in my thinking.

The physical time is fixed but the realising time or absolute time is not fixed, it varies from man to man or person to person.

Every living thing maintains a time and that time is a variable time depends on the thinking of different things or body to body. Actually the time is different for every zone of the Earth and for different person living in different zone maintains different clock. If we follow the different time then our thinking will be different. As an example: The condition that you think one hour and I think it as thirty minutes. So when I think one hour is left to do the work you will think that two hours is left for the work.

 The reader must have to read and understand carefully about the two types of time. For that I am trying my best to explain in deep on the next pages.

In the previous page I want to say about my experience and thinking about time as we feel minute into seconds.

Now in more small cases we divide the second into milliseconds. This is the physical time and we keep a clock in our room and we make the hour hand, the minute hand also the total objective of my book is given. Later on this book I will discuss the whole matter.

From a long time many people think about the time. People prepare calendar to remember time or happenings of something in our life. Actually in every period of an emperor it was essential to remember the happenings of everything throughout his lifetime and for that they need to see the Moon and the Sun. Some people took the rotation of moon around the Earth as a unit of year. Some people took the rotation of the Earth about the Sun as the unit of year. After taking this long time interval as a year we took the next rotation of the Earth about its own axis as one day. Then we divide one day into hour and one hour into minutes and one minute into seconds and these three hands moving always to see the time. We mainly compare the other things happening with respect to the happening of movement of clock and that helps us to feel about the time.

People of ancient time use different things to remember his time. But if all the people use the time differently then there may be different problems and so we create international timeline or time zone. Now if you want to know the time of individual then you have to ask individually about the time what he or she follows.

A person who rises at 6 a.m. and starts working keeping a watch in his hand which shows one minute as thirty seconds can feel that the time goes faster than a person whose watch is dividing as one minute equals sixty seconds. So the first person's thinking of time expands or gives him more life than the second. If another person keeps his watch as one minute equals to fifteen seconds then he will think that the time goes faster though all the time the physical time is same. Time is that which you feel but not that physical time which we fixed. Time of a human, an elephant, or other animals are different for their different feelings. But we divide the large time of rotation of earth or small time as rotation of electrons as fixed to find or generalise our time. When we require short measurement of happenings then smallest division of time is used. When large measurement of happenings is required then largest division of time is used. As millisecond and decades are smaller and larger time span we can take respectively.

Time variable in every position of a mobile is different. That is for different location, the time of a mobile is different. If anyone can set his own time span in his mobile then he can be in fast or slow as per his choice. But we can track the person with different time set by radar like instrument very smoothly if the position of the mobile differs.

Thinking (T) with time (t) can change the future of a game playing anywhere. It is by the axial thinking with respect to our brain. It can be denoted by ("dT/dt"=same and greater). For the same time interval if the thinking is same then there may be a clash. If someone can think greater with time than other then he can say the future of the person who thinks less in time. In mathematical point of view dT/dt>>1 represents the thinking rate higher than one that is more, more greater than 1 which means the person thinks very fast with time.

Again dT/dt<<1 represents the thinking is lower or the person is thinking slowly with time change, here the thinking is more, more less than 1.

When a game is playing in Delhi then a person can see directly from Kolkata and minimum time taken by the light to go Delhi to Kolkata is more than the thinking of someone who can see the match and its result's proper statistics and say the result of the match before. If any man on the ground can see the match has a link with the man in the home then the match result can be said easily before the match is over. This process can be done through mobile phone because to play a ball one after other, players take more time than the time taken by mobile.

If a person can think in time and another person can think in less time, then the person who thinks in less can say the answer first than the other. Here also if a man who thinks first can say the result of the match first. This is for dT/dt of second is greater than dT/dt of the first.

The thinking rate per time is used as dT/dt and we can use the time rate per thinking as dt/dT. These two are related to each other. In case of dT/dt we can think or find our thinking rate with time rate. In case of dt/dT we can think the time changing rate by our thinking. I am telling here both the two things. Time changing rate is different for different thinkers and also thinking rate is different with time.

At first we fixed our dt/dT then we started to think and our thinking rate with that time change (dT/dt) can be found. The thinking rate differs as the rate of time with thinking differs. So as many people as there are the thinking rate are there and for that thinking of time also. If we can give same time (physical time) to everyone then the person who thinks faster can give the answer faster because his thinking time with respect to given time is faster.

<u>**Difference between time and thinking**</u>

Time and thinking are different as we can realise the time but we can't realise our thinking, I want to mean we can't know that if someone is thinking or not from outside directly but can assume it. Time can be seen from watch but thinking can be seen possibly by computer attached with our brain.

There may be no overlapping of time but there may be overlapping in thinking in our brain. I want to say that our thinking of one thing overlaps with other thinking within a certain time and that thinking can't be memorised.

Time has a physical appearance in our daily life but thinking may not have any physical appearance in our daily life.

Thinking may be zero but physical time or the time changing in a clock may not be zero. In large scale time may be year and small scale it may be milliseconds. Thinking can be of three stages as high, low and medium and we can plot it by computer after adjusting our brain in computer.

Thinking of time depends on the person and thinking also depends on the person but physical time always different than thinking time.

For different person the time or physical time is same (may be same) but thinking time is different (may not same).

(1)

(2)

In the above figure the figure (1) shows the physical time and figure (2) shows the thinking

<u>**Relation between time and thinking**</u>

Actually time is nothing but realisation by thinking. When we see a clock then we can realise the small change in second hand of the clock and we can think it as one second, but if you feel much less in your digital clock then you can think the less time. So time is nothing but the thinking. In earlier times we did not know clock so we use

In case of a faster person the time goes fast and in case of an idle person the time goes slow and in case of normal person time goes as the clock he follows.

As many thinking are there as many time of thinking there are. Number of thinking is equals to number of time, or feelings of time equals to number of thinking.

Only living bodies can feel the time and can think. So thinking of time is different or same for different living bodies. The thinking of living bodies is same or different.

The thinking of time is the cause of thinking the change of time, as we can see time as we think the time.

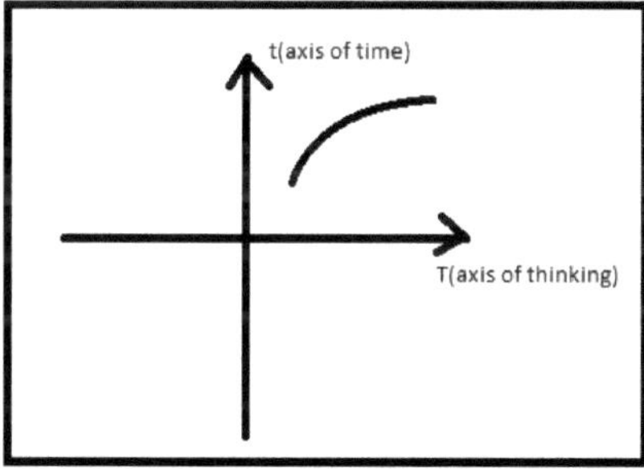

The above figure shows the time and thinking graph for the relation with time and thinking, taking two positive axes.

<u>**Rate of change of thinking with respect to time**</u>

Rate of change of thinking with respect to time is denoted by dT/dt , where T stands for thinking and t stands for time. When $\Delta t \to 0$ then $\Delta T / \Delta t$ =dT/dt as we know from general calculus. Now if dT/dt>1 then the person thinking high with respect to time. If dT/dt<1 then the person is thinking less with respect to time. Now most of us think with time as it gives dT/dt=1. The person with dT/dt>>1 can say the happenings before the occurrence than the other person.

Normal person thinks with respect to time generally but sometimes we think fast with time and sometimes slow with time. It depends upon the work a person is doing and the person can think as his or her need with time.

Intelligent person can think faster and mad person can also think faster but the lazy person or dull person or who likes to live in simple life can think slower or with time.

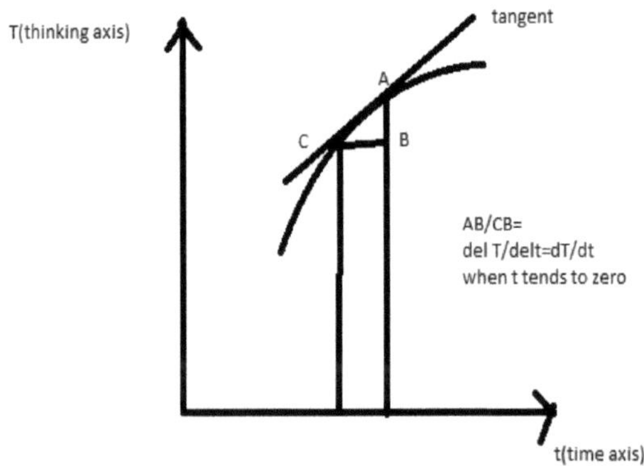

Thinking of time with respect to time is shown here in the above figure. Rate of change of thinking of time or thinking with respect to physical time or simply the time can be seen in this figure.

<u>Now what is thinking?</u>

Actually when we say about a thing then we say that by our thinking and memory, so if we say the answer quick then we can say that we are thinking fast. But if we say about the thing taking long time then also we think and if the long thinking gives the correct answer then we say that the long thinking is rigid and proper. So time bound question or simple question answers are the measurement of thinking. As far as I don't give the thinking of a man who can't say anything, we will proceed more easily about question answer as the thinking ability. Though the reader can approach with the help of computer to measure our thinking but the relationship of thinking and time must be same.

When we simplify a problem or when we solve some problems then we use our brain memory and power to solve that. This power to solve the problem is thinking power. The thinking is the power by which we do solve our problems or we can give answers to many question from our memory or from our intelligence.

<u>Increase of time</u>

We can increase our time. The time of one hour can be increased to two hours if we do all the work of two hours in one hour then our time in hand will show us that we save one hour and that will increase our time.

Just start to count 12 hours as one day then you will live double than you normally live. In everyday you work fast and complete the whole 24 hours work in 12 hours you can find that you are in a clock or you are maintaining a clock with 12 hours a day.

Actually increase of time means utilising the time as many ways as possible so that we can do more work in less time.

<u>Thinking of time increased</u>

Thinking of time can be increased by other or thinking time can be increased by other, but that is not equal to the increase of time span by us. The two types of increasing are different but they have a common relation. You are getting 365 days in a year but after four years you can get 366 days in a year so your time of year increased but if you think slowly and work like a lazy one then you can feel that 365 days as 366 days or if you are doing the work fast then the time will go fast and you can feel the time span as 364 days. So the relation of fixed time and mental time helps to increase the time when the fixed time 365 days increased to 366 days and we work fast.

Decrease of time

When we want to go slow then we decrease our time. Then we take two hours to do a work of one hour and normally our time decreases and we are in slow movement, we are late as we decrease our time we feel that time is not going but we are following less time. In old age or to solve a hard problem in our mind it is required to decrease our time.

Everyone want to utilise the life or to win in his life or to live like his way and for that we must utilise our time span , if we decrease our time then we can feel that we are living a long life but we can do less work as if we increase our time.

Thinking of time decreased

When we get the year as 365 days and after four years we get 366 days then time of a year increased but after that 366 days we get 365 days so time of the year decreased and if we do work slowly then remaining time decreases and our life decreased. So when the time of year decreased with time of thinking then thinking of time decreased.

Relative time

Time is relative with thinking of different person or different living or non living objects.

Different person can think differently, so from the one thinking we can see or maintain a time and other thinking we maintain the other time. So for that time of one person is relative to other. The time of one person is relative to the time of other. Here the two person looks at different time division and for that their time are relative time. When the two persons can think of same time then their relative time is zero. If two persons follow different time interval then their time difference is the relative time's value.

If one person is thinking very faster than other then the person who thinks fast can feel faster time than other and we can see the relative time. Here the relative time is their time difference.

The time of two persons is different as they follow the different clock. Like one person think with respect to a clock where one rotation is equal to 12 minutes and other person thinks the one rotation of a minute hand is 60 minutes.

Figures given below show two kinds of clocks in which we can see the different time as relative time.

this is one type of clock where every small part shows a minute.

This is a general clock we use

<u>**Relative thinking**</u>

Thinking of a person is relative with respect to various circumstances or various outer objects. Thinking of a person is relative to a fixed thing can't be possible but it can be found out with respect to nature. Different natural conditions are the causes of different types of thinking. Similarly different lifestyle of a man changed the thinking of that man.

One man's thinking is relative to other person's thinking, if the two persons think same then the person whose thinking is with more confidence can be taken and it is relatively higher than the other.

If you have no clock and you can't compare certain changes then also you can think and you will think about the happenings by comparing it with your own body activities even you can't see then you will compare with your feelings.

The thinking is relative as the thinking of different person is different and also the thinking of same person in different place or in different time is different. So with respect to one type of thinking the other type of thinking is relative thinking.

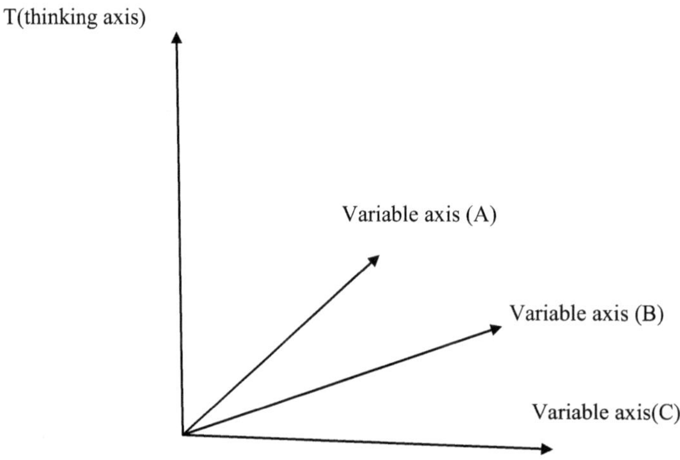

Here in the figure we see that thinking is relative with other variables.

<u>Relative thinking is respected value but relative time is not respected only, it is relative also</u>

I want to mean thinking is respected but it is not relative as we can't compare two different thinking but the respected thinking of a man can be said as relative thinking. Time is relative as we compare two different times and also it is respected as we can see different measurement of time in feeling of same person. So it is also respected.

The relative thinking is the respected value which is found by fixing some other things as constant but thinking about time or simply time is a respected value and for two or more time we get a relative value.

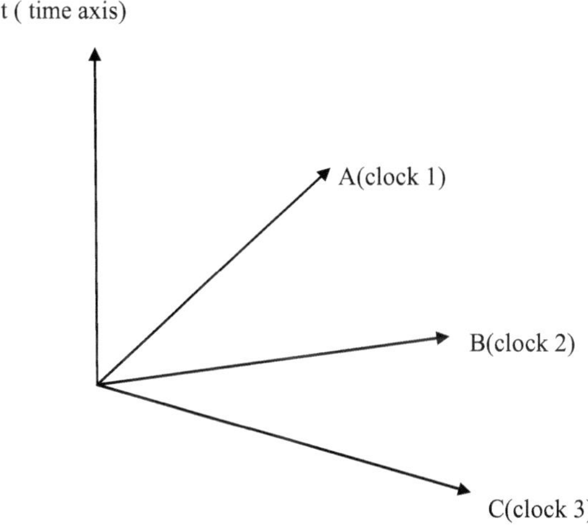

In the above figure the time depends on three different clocks where the time is respected value and relative value.

Real time machine

The time machines are the machines which records the incidents time by time or with time. Our various recorders are those examples. Various places show the time machines also. Radio, TV set, computer, mobile can store different incident of past and these things are time machines because with particular time the machine shows you a particular incident. But those time machines are not running, if we see the whole world, then all the different places are the examples of different time wise occurrence in our world and if we go time by time then we can find a time machine. Like we want to start our journey from Africa to Asia to America then our time machine like journey will take us from less develop countries to modern countries and it will a journey of future time for the people of African countries.

In the reverse we can go from India to America we will see the future time occurrence and to Africa we can see the past of Indian people or India. All the modern things are present in America, which are not present in India but after sometime it will come to India, so India's future is America's present. Again if we go to Africa then we actually go to our past. This is the actual real life time machine we can see always.

If the past things are stored in a computer and we follow them and always think them then we can go to our past and it is by an artificial machine and also called a time machine.

I don't want to say the time machine by which we can go to our future by going faster than light or other ways with the help of the knowledge of physics.

The real time machine are given in the picture which is the computer, most modern.

So the whole world is a time machine where we are living is the real time and other with different position is given as past or future according to their occurrences.

In this world everything is attached with time. For one person's time we get a particular time difference and for other person's it is different. For that there is two or more time machine according to the time. If in a clock one rotation is 12 minutes then 5 rotations is equal to one hour. Here a time maintaining instrument shows the time different than normal time maintaining instrument. So taking 12 minutes as one unit we can set a machine and the machine will record many things with that time. Various such time instruments can be made. Though there are all the living or non living bodies maintains the different or same time machines.

<u>We always in the present tense in our thinking but always in past in other real life</u>

When we see anything then we see the past so what we think after looking, is a thinking on past occurrence. We can always in past because we can see the figure after lights fall on it and we think in our mind always the present and we are prepare for the future for the thinking.

We are in our future in our thinking or we can think about our future but the thinking time can be negative sense also. When we think about our past then our thinking time is with negative sense.

Thinking about the past is done by thinking about the negative time of thinking that is if we think about 2000 year in 2022 year then we are thinking the negative time of thinking or negative thinking happens.

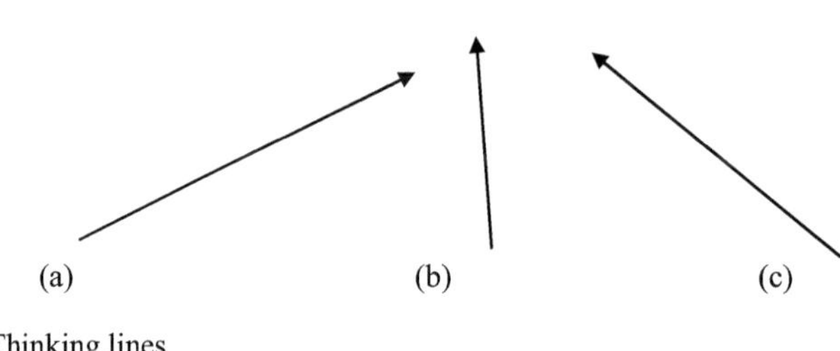

Thinking lines

Negative sense of time or negative time

When we go to our past then our negative sense of time comes and it is the negative time. From a fixed position the negative time can be counted. But thinking of time can't be negative because the thinking always in positive side. Again if the person can always think his surrounding state as past then he or she can feel the negative time or negative sense of time

Zero time or without the starting of time

If we are in the sense after a sleep then we feel the zero time. Actually we can start to think and also start to respect the changes with one another and I will say that this is the starting time of feeling by thinking.

<u>**Time is always positive**</u>

Time is always in positive direction. It is a strictly increasing function. This time is physical time or the time we see in the clock. But the time which we feel or the thinking of time is increasing and decreasing and fixed all of these three (positive, negative, zero).

<u>Positive sense of time</u>

When we think about the increase of time that is about future then positive sense of time comes.

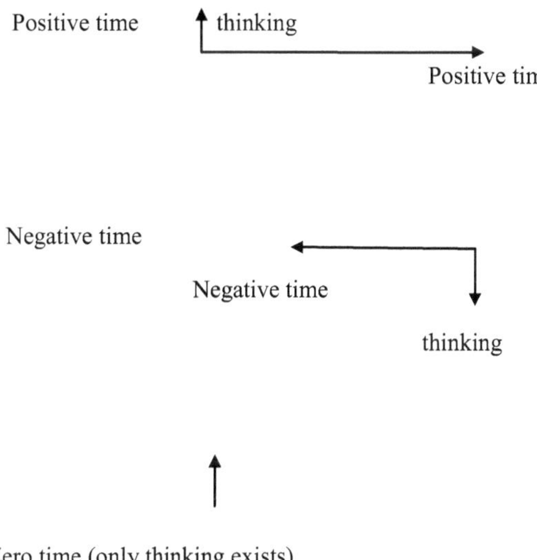

<u>**We can relate artificial intelligence with time**</u>

Artificial intelligence is related with time. If our thinking time is less than our physical time then we are more intelligent. So if we can give the thinking time of a computer very low that means if the computer can think in short time than us then the computer will more intelligent than us .

So we will produce information to a computer such that it gives the answer of any question before other, then by our artificial help the computer can be artificially intelligent. Many people are attached with a computer in a certain time can help the computer to be more intelligent than any other. Here the time zone helps the computer and link of the computer with some intelligent people help the computer.

If we take the help of feeling time high then we will be artificially more intelligent. Actually if someone can do the work faster than other then he or she is more artificially intelligent.

Thinking is dependent with other things like smelling, looking, hearing, touching, tasting. So our senses help the thinking to find out something or to realise time. If the realisation of time is very fast then the thinker is artificially more intelligent or if any computer can realise the time fast then he can give the answer quickly and we get an artificially more intelligent thing. The other thing is that thinking can go with only one variable also.

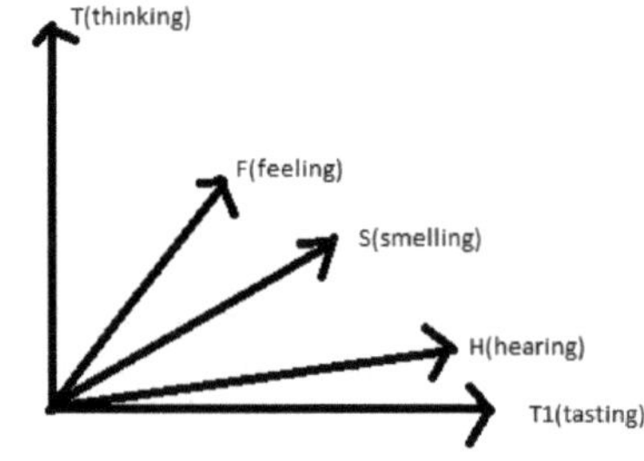

thinking is depending on other things

there are five things which is responsible for realisation of a thing. They are feeling(F), smelling(S), hearing(H), tasting(T1) and thinking(T). These five main things is responsible for feeling time also.

Time in space compared by looking the objects of space from earth by a telescope

The time on space

The time on space is different than the time on the Earth. In the space we compare any movement with the movement of other planetary objects but that time is not our consideration. I will say the time what we feel after we observe other objects by our thinking and that time is the real time.

Taking the Sun's direction as fixed we can set a time. Here we will see the other planet's movement in an interval as a time gap, which is our time in space for that fixed system on space. This time is different for man to man or observer to observer. Now if the observer is changes from animal to animal then their feeling of time differs.

The time on the Earth

Time on the Earth can be different for different region for the physical time but can also be same for different minded people. The people who maintains same time for their work they can be in same time. So in the Earth we are also in different time zone but of same time with thinking.

When we are in our planet then what we see we can compare that with time changes and we follow a time zone. Again if we think about something with our own feeling of time then also time changes but it is thinking time.

The time on other planet

The time on the other planet is different for different beings but can be same if we maintain the same time with the survivors of other planets. Here the two location of the planets be different but the thinking of the two planet's survivors are same and so their time of thinking may same or time is taken as same for the two planets.

The time of the other planet is with different time zone but the thinking time can be same with the thinking time of the Earth. Sometime the time of thinking is different or same, sometime the thinking time is different or same.

<u>**Biological time of each body or living beings**</u>

The main thing is about the time is the biological time. The clock which our body maintains is the biological clock. Everyday our body takes food and we sleep in proper time that time is our biological time. In 24 hours of a day we sleep in a particular time and we eat food for our requirements and for digestion sleeping and working is necessary. Also for our brain we have to take rest. The time what our body follows is the time of our biological clock.

The main thing is that we can control our biological clock by our thinking and by our time of thinking or time rate with thinking rate.

The biological clock of different person is different. All the persons in a country maintain a particular clock and do their work so the biological clock of a person differs with the biological clock of other person of another country.

The biological clock of every person with different jobs is different. The most important thing is biological clock of every person changes time to time according to his or her thinking of lifestyle.

All the living organisms have a biological clock and they maintain that clock. Different animals have different biological clock but most of the time the group of same animals in a country maintain same biological clock.

Each plant maintains a biological clock to live. The plants in different position maintain the different biological clock. Actually in plants we can see the biological clock proper because they maintain it properly. We can make an experiment with the plant which sleeps after sunset.

If we think about our daily routine then we can change our biological clock by our thinking of time. Our time always runs but our thinking also runs which is sometime faster than time so if we use the thinking then we can change our biological clock.

If the biological clock is going wrong then we can manage the clock by our thinking of time with change of physical time respect to our biological clock.

If biological clock is different then we must follow that clock in our thinking. If the thinking clock hampers the biological clock then there may be some disturbances in our life.

Various plants and animals follow different biological clock and as a result their body maintain the time differently. Even an ant does its work in time by maintaining the biological clock.

Duration of time is same but as the feeling of time changes the working time can be different. As the working time is different the biological clock is different if we biologically fixed some time for our biological life then to fix our time with the work of our biological cause like sleeping mainly then that time fixes the biological time. Many works are there for our body which maintain our biological clock. Like go to a bathroom in a fixed time, do some physical exercise for our body in a fixed time, walking everyday in a fixed time are all the biological time.

<u>**Time span on our thinking**</u>

We can set different time span by our thinking. For same physical time we can think different time interval. Like one hour is equal to one minute to someone. Time is totally a feeling and so that if you feel the time span better then you can utilise it better. One year is 365 days approximately but if you use the year thinking very fast then you have more time or you can work much within the one year. We can expand the time interval or time span by setting the clock into different time division or different mode.

We can divide 1 second into 10 small seconds or 30 divisions as we want to divide the duration. Again we can divide 1 hour into 36 divisions. In these types of dividing the time is spanned and we get a large time for the sense of time gap is very high. Here we are fast that is we think the time fast. The physical time that we see is divided by our thinking is used for time span. Now thinking span is different when we take same time and think about more things the thinking may overlap on one another. So we take time span to span our thinking time for not to the overlapping of thinking. Different types of thinking in the same time can cause the overlapping of thinking and for that we must take more time to types of thinkings.

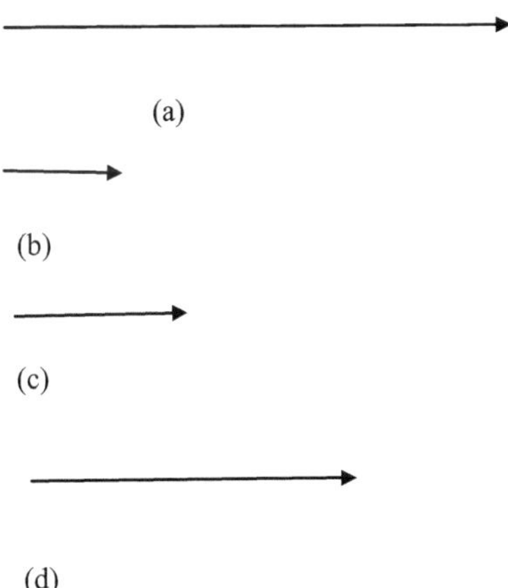

(a)

(b)

(c)

(d)

The figures above show the different time span in our thinking

<u>Gaps between the two times or two types of time</u>

There must be some gaps in between two times or there are infinite division in between two times but the division can be countable and dense.

If we divide our time as per our own choice then we always find a gap between two times. Since there are gaps we can get a chance to do or shift one work to other.

Two types of time also have many gaps. In between two types of time we see the gaps, if the gaps are not seen then two types of time overlaps each other.

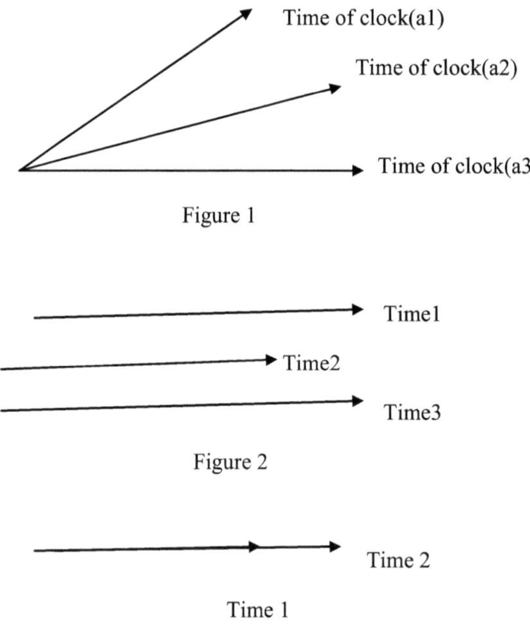

Here figure 1 shows the different time. Figure 2 shows the different time but with different phase and figure 3 shows the overlapping time.

<u>**Gaps between two types of thinking**</u>

Thinking of time is with gaps. That means there are gaps between thinking of time for a person and also for different person. For same person thinking of time is different by time to time. This thinking of time is different for different person because their thinking in a same time is different and so there is gap in between two persons thinking of time. Sometime we think one hour as one minute and sometime we think one day as one year. These thinking of two types of time have a gap at least for separating those thinking, otherwise our mind can't realise it. If we think two types of time then there must be at least one gap for a single man and for different person the gaps are there in between two types of thinking of time always. Time of different person in their thinking is different and so there are gaps.

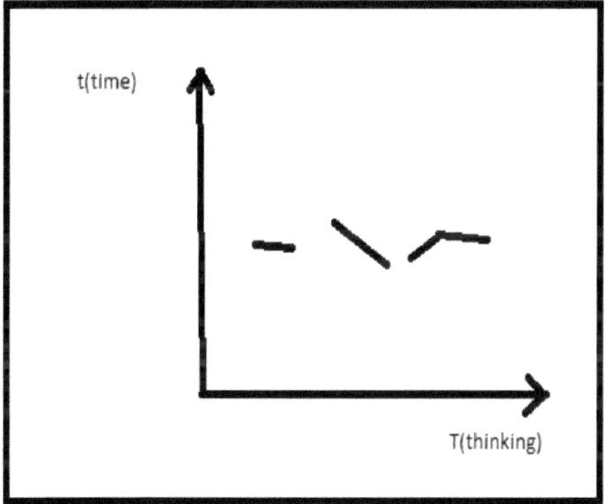

Here we see the gaps in the thinking in above the figure

This picture given below shows the universal time and the construction of equivalent time or universal time is discussed here.

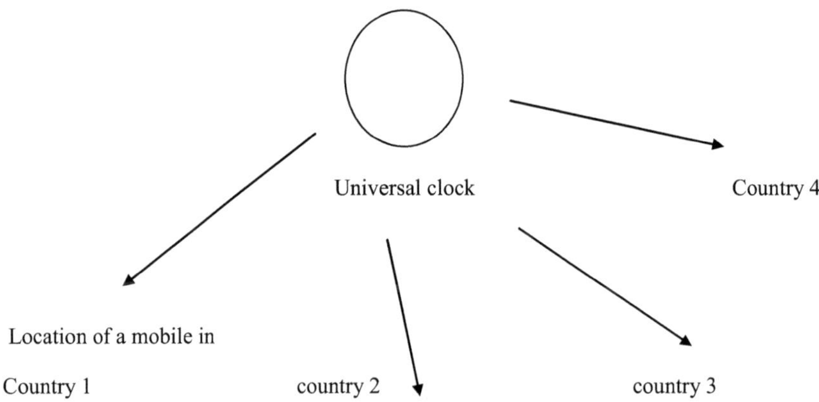

<u>To construct an equivalent time for all</u>

Giving a same clock to all the mobile can make or control all the persons as a unit or can give information to everyone in a same time.

It is very easy to understand that we can set a universal time for all or for some zone to make the relation with one another. For the same time we can do a certain work but my point of view is that we can use our time as per our ability to do the work in our life or day to day life. There may be a problem to other who wants to be active in others time and so we will construct a time where the duration of time changes time to time in all of our thinking. If we do all that way then we can go in upward direction with using our thinking of time.

Actually in every zone the collective people work with time but the person who thinks better of time is the gainer. So for us we have to follow the time which we think that is thinking of time. The time which we can feel in our mind must be greater than the physical time which we can see from clock or other things.

So it is necessary to construct a universal time or equivalent time for all. Now if we fix some time interval as fixed and all the computers link together with a fixed time then they will run together. Then we can hack other computer by one linked computer but if we create different time for different computers and one fixed time for all the electronic computers then by using different division of time for a fixed computer we can secure our work in computer.

<u>To keep your system safe different time setting is essential</u>

Setting the clock of a system different can help to keep you safe from other who wants to know your system.

If every person can set his or her known thing in a particular time value then no one can take his or her thing. That is the cause of a computer to memorise many things with time but the difference between computer and us is that we can use thinking of time but computer uses the physical time. If we introduce our thinking time and computer then the computer can't be hacked. If our thinking can store the item we see in our memory with the help of thinking time then after some thinking of different time setting in memory to remember our things we can change the thinking time but the user or owner always knows the thing, other can't.

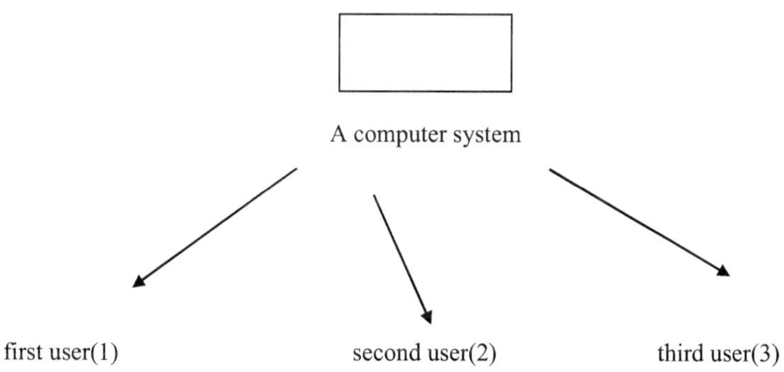

Here all the three users use the computers which are linked with a same computer but their positional time or zone wise time is different than linking time.

<u>Thinking of the time can change a person</u>

Thinking of a person helps to think about time and thinking about time change the person. If you are thinking the time going fast then you work fast and reversely. So the main thing is your thinking about time. The real time which we see can never change us but the time in our thinking can change us. From a slow person or slow thinker we can get a result but the thinker who thinks fast about time can help us from danger if possible.

If you think about something then the thinking result will give an output value which can be useful to you. Now if we concern about the change around us or if we concern about time change then we can do our work before time.

Thinking of time can change the world. As the people of a country think about their work within a short time the country grows fast and every person of that country get facilities from their work.

When a person can't think about time then his life can't change easily because thinking about time and working is the cause of growth. Here the person only works but not thinking about time so he can go but he can't feel about the time. This is very good for a person when he works without looking at time but the time concentration for any work can give success.

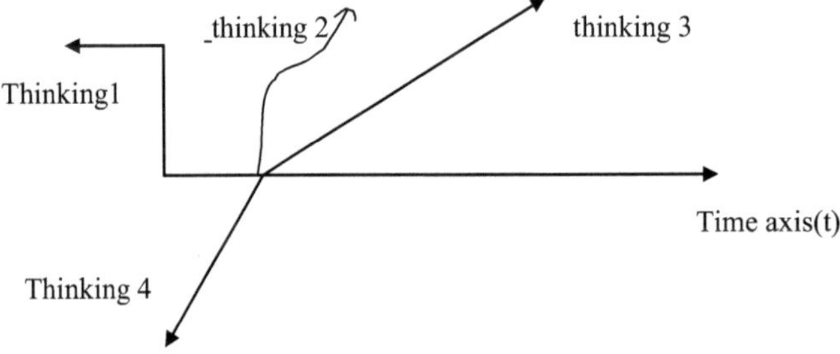

From different thinking the time is different. Also the reverse for same time thinking is different.

<u>Time can't change the thinking but thinking can change the realisation of time</u>

The physical time or the fixed time duration can't change our thinking but the thinking can change the thinking about time or sense of time. The thinking of time can change all the realisation of time and we can think different time duration.

Time can't change our thinking directly but if we wish to change our thinking with time then we can. Thinking can change the feelings of time as the time is a dependable thing on our thinking. Anyone can think the time interval as his or her own choice. Someone thinks one hour as a unit of time and other can think 15 minutes as a unit of time. So for different one the time is different and for them they can create their own clock to follow .

<u>Realisation of time for a rigid body</u>

For a rigid body there is no time of realisation that means rigid body can only has the physical time. In the case of a rigid body the time of its life span or time of decaying can be found.

A rigid body or body without life also maintains the time. The time of movement of electron is one kind of time related movement. Actually we compare our time with the time of fixed rigid body but it is difficult to think that our body is made up with rigid parts but our mind where thinking happens is a sensational part. So the two types of time are always unequal.

The sensational part is also varies from animals to animals and so the real rigid time is not fixed for use value. The use value of time is more important than physical value.

The rigid body changes due to change in nature sometimes, but it maintains the natural time which we feel by observing that rigid body.

Discussion about many things on time and thinking

Invisible time

Without any change if we can think about anything then thinking can't say the time or time can't be found. If we think without any other change then the time will invisible. I want to say if all the clock stops for a while and we are thinking then thinking time is invisible, because if the clock stops then thinking may not stop, and we see the time of thinking is null physically but original time is going in our thinking. That is invisible time.

The thinking is always invisible but has an existence to feel the happenings like time interval or other things.

<u>Different time for same person</u>

Different realisation of different changes can give different times. So time can be different for same person with different thinking, as he can think with respect to the change of different clock's different movement and different time.

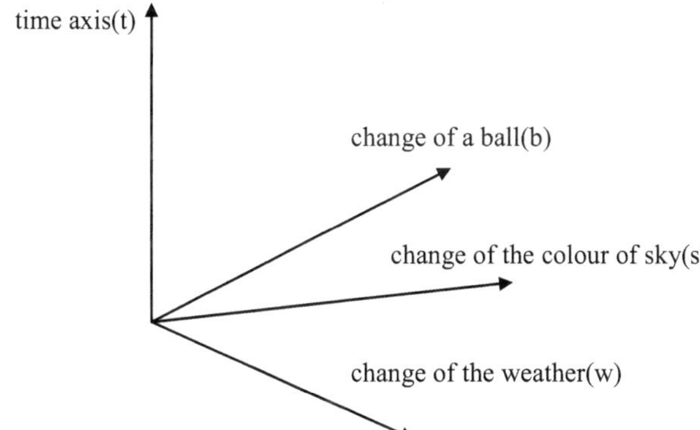

<u>**Types of curve**</u>

If the thinking of time in our world is taken as physical time then it is a continuous variable of simple curve but the thinking of time is also a curve with or without continuity because if someone thinks about a time then sometime he can forget to look the time and it seems to him or her that time stops.

There is a close relationship between thinking time and physical time. The thinking time is greater than physical time means the person thinks the shorter time interval than the usual time interval.

<u>**Types of time curve for different person**</u>

We can get different time curve for different person. As we get different time or physical time curve of a person we also get different thinking of time curve for different person. Here the two curves are different. For physical time curve the time interval is same but for thinking of time related curve is with different time intervals.

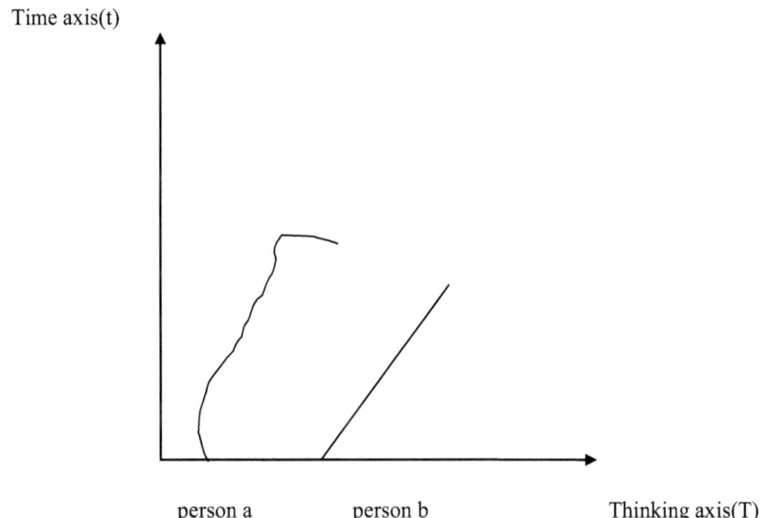

thinking of different person in some time interval is shown here in the figure

<u>**Boundary points of time**</u>

Time has one boundary point the lower boundary point but no upper boundary point but lower boundary point is not fixed. Lower boundary point is the starting point of count. When we start to count time then it is the lower boundary point but it has no end. Actually time has no boundary points upper or lower though we can get lower boundary point as our choice but no last point. But in real physical time there is a last time when no one will be to measure time, and the students of science can give the proper description of time which we know. But in my point of view is the thinking of time, the time which we realise.

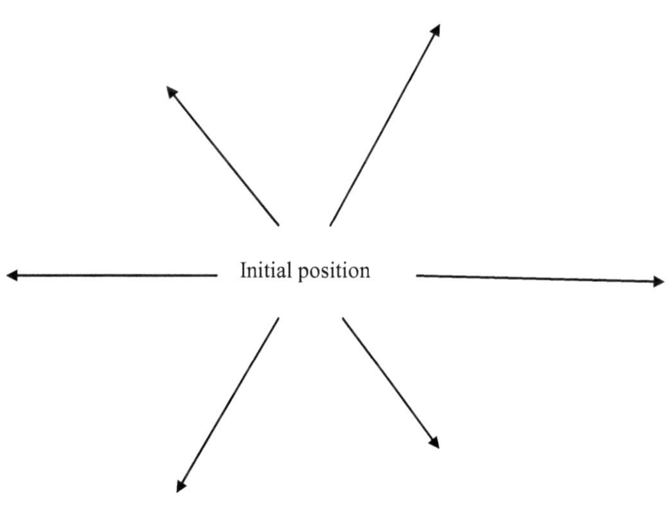

Times are like that picture above

<u>**Boundary points of thinking**</u>

Thinking has no boundary points. As there is no starting of a thinking or ending of thinking we can't find the boundary points. Some one can't express thinking but they think about a thing, which is invisible.

When we start to think then the starting point of thinking found but we can't initialize the thinking time of start as it is an internal thing also for the ending point it is true. The physical time of starting to think can be found but actual thinking time can't be found. Thinking is a thing which can't be kept into a condition it is an automatic process which have no starting or ending point.

Thinking in different time is like that

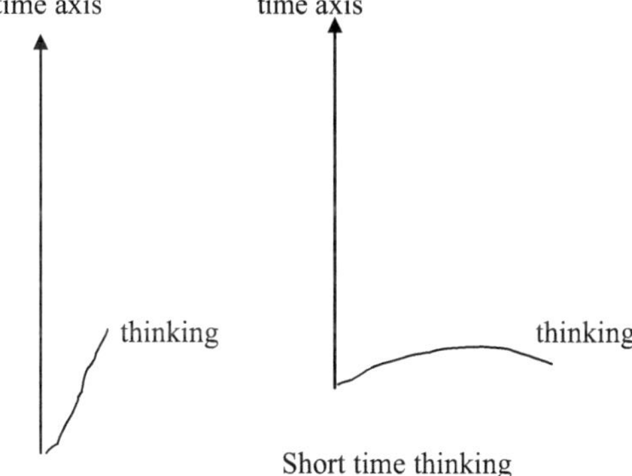

Short time thinking and long time thinking

There are two type of thinking mainly seen in our life. One is short time thinking and other is long time thinking. When we think in a short time then it is short time thinking and when we take a long time then we get a result after thinking in long time and that thinking type is long time thinking. I am discussing it later.

Short time thinking and its effect

When we think for a short time interval of our physical time then we say it short time thinking. Within a short time we can use our thinking and that thinking is short time thinking. Actually the time taken is short and thinking is high. Many cases are there where a person can die in that type of thinking in old age, because in old age we can't do it all the time. The effect of short time thinking is very helpful but only the great thinker or the intelligent persons can give the better result.

A young person is helpful for short time thinking and an old one is helpful for long time thinking. So if we take the help of a young and an old person to do a work with their thinking then the answer will better or the result will be better.

Though a young man can do both types of thinking well but the old aged person will take the help of their experiences to think long time thinking.

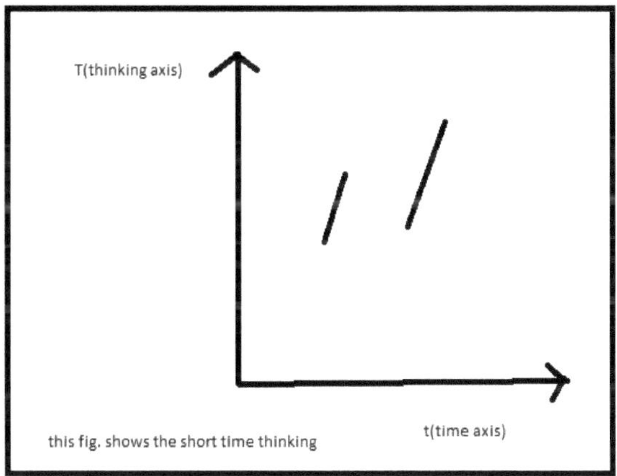

Short time thinking with respect to normal time is shown in the above figure.

Long time thinking and its effect

When we think about a thing for a long time then it is long time thinking. We think for long time that is for long physical time then our thinking is long time thinking. Most of the time we can use long time to solve a harder problem and that type of thinking is long type thinking. When we think for a long time or the thinking goes fast but after a long physical time we can get the result then we say that it is the long time thinking.

The effect of long time thinking is good for us but sometime it makes us slow. If we think slowly then our result comes slow but if the resulting time is short then we can't use long time thinking.

The aged person can think slowly most of the time. The younger person thinks also slowly when the problem is hard. So according to solve the problem we use long time thinking.

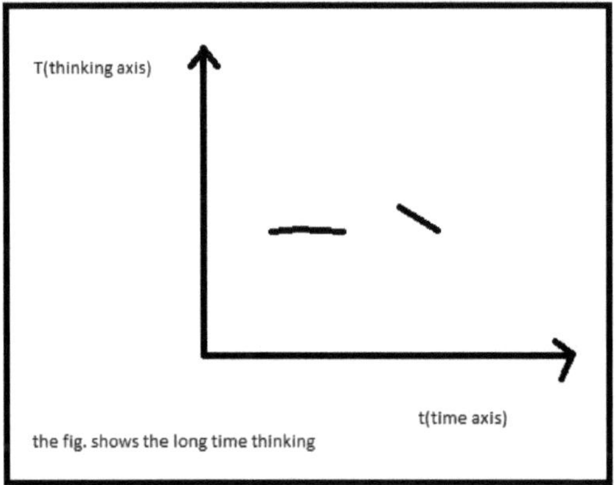

Long time thinking with respect to normal time is shown in the above figure.

Loosing of time

The time which is not used by us is lost every time. Actually when you or we are not thinking then the time is going, more properly when we are in sleep then we are not doing anything but time goes in outside of our brain or physical time goes. This may be time loss. But actually time never lost. The thinking time loses. If you don't think in your brain about anything and if you do not work with time then time of thinking is lost.

You can't get back the previous time. The time is running always and we can't get back to the past or we can't go to our past in reality but in virtual world we may go. We can't find out the time which we lost. The time in front of us is future and which we feel is past. Present time is so nearer to our eyes or feelings that it goes within a moment. So rate of change of time with respect to time has a view and rate of change of time with respect to thinking has a view.

Use of time by under develop countries and developing countries

Under develop countries can't use the time properly, they loss time. If all the people can do their work on time or do in less time, then their country goes fast and the country becomes developed. So under develop countries can't use their time proper but developing countries can use the time as they can do by following developed countries. Use of time is the tool to be a good, modern country. Actually computer has come to the earth to minimise our effort and we can calculate everything in shorter time. So time and we is related with the great machine like computer. The developing countries use computers less than developed countries.

<u>**Use of time by develop countries**</u>

Develop countries uses the time as much as possible. Also they use time to develop themselves such that they can use the minimum time for a work. Actually the time is same for all the universal things but the realisation of time makes the difference. The develop countries uses the short time division and do their work in short time and get the result of their work proper before other countries. That is the difference which makes a distance from develop countries to under develop countries/developing countries.

The main thing i say from the first to the end that the time is the time which you /we feel not the time we fixed as year. We must set different time span for our work respect and by that time we can change the world.

If the calculator is not there then we can't use less time to calculate we have to use much time to calculate and the time will loss. This is the use of time. All the develop countries use computers, electronic gadgets to save time. The time which they saved is used for other work. So the time is not important rather the utility of time. If we use time proper then our country, our world will grow fast and we will be all developed.

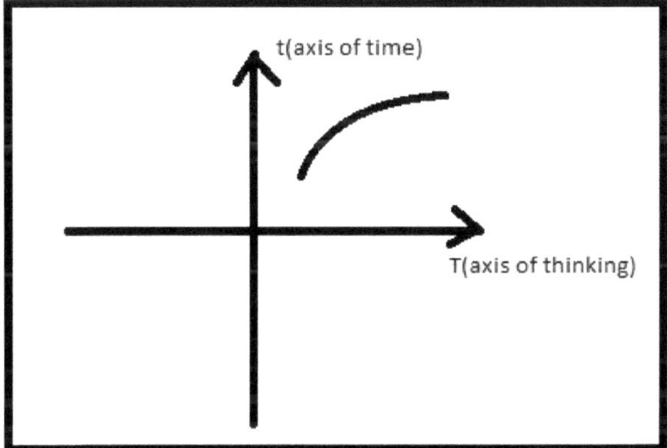

One simple figure is given here to describe the relation of time and thinking .Below I am giving different figures to describe the relation between time and thinking.

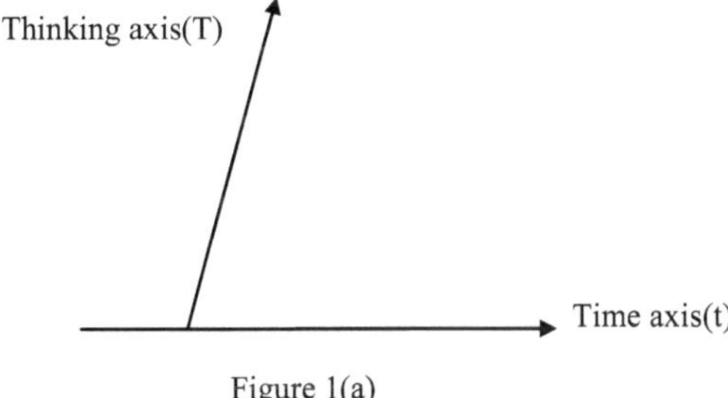

Figure 1(a)

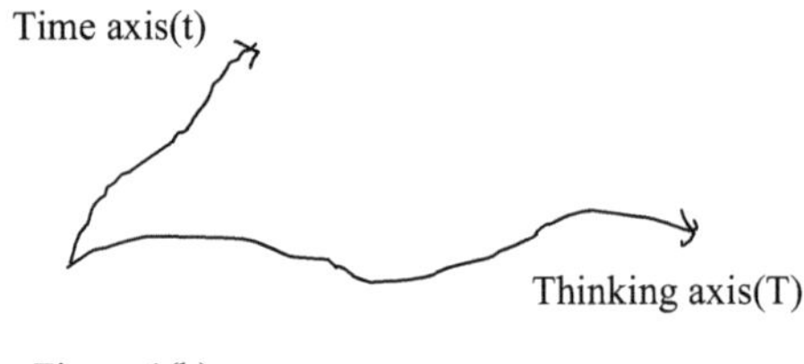

Figure 1(b)

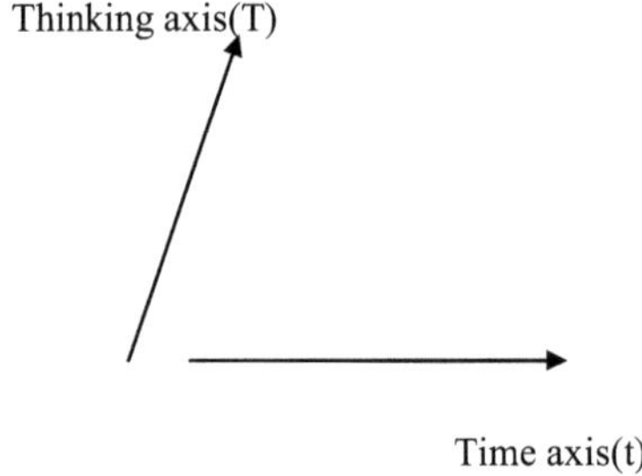

Sometimes the thinking happens without time, and so there is a gap at first in the above figure

We are related with time

Thinking of time relates us. Some of us use the time very fast and some of us not very fast. So the thinking time of someone is the complement of the thinking time of other may be.

If someone is thinking fast then he thinks the time fast so there is someone who is with opposite thinking has the thinking time slow, and we say that those two person are complement to each other.

One person's short time thinking can hamper other person's long time thinking. So an aged person and a small child can think the time oppositely. If they can be kept together then we can see that two time of thinking are different for those two.